THE VILLAGE SINGS

A very happy Christmas,
to my good friend
Delwydd Jones

Gabriel Fitzmaurice

OTHER BOOKS BY GABRIEL FITZMAURICE

Poetry in English
Rainsong (Beaver Row Press, Dublin 1984)
Road to the Horizon (Beaver Row Press, Dublin 1987)
Dancing Through (Beaver Row Press, Dublin 1990)
The Father's Part (Story Line Press, Oregon 1992)
The Space Between: New and Selected Poems 1984–1992
 (Cló Iar Chonnachta, Conamara 1993)

Poetry in Irish
Nocht (Coiscéim, Dublin 1989)
Ag Síobhshiúl Chun An Rince (Coiscéim, Dublin 1995)

Children's Poetry in English
The Moving Stair (The Kerryman, Tralee 1989)
The Moving Stair (enlarged edition — Poolbeg Press, Dublin 1993)
But Dad! (Poolbeg Press, Dublin 1995)

Children's Poetry in Irish
Nach Iontach Mar Atá (Cló Iar Chonnachta, Conamara 1994)

Translation
The Purge (A translation of *An Phurgóid* by Mícheál Ó hAirtnéide —
 Beaver Row Press, Dublin 1989)
Poems I Wish I'd Written: Translations from the Irish
 (Cló Iar Chonnachta, Conamara 1996)

Editor
The Flowering Tree/ An Crann Faoi Bhláth (contemporary poetry in Irish
 with verse translations,) *with Declan Kiberd* — Wolfhound Press,
 Dublin 1991
Between the Hills and Sea: Songs and Ballads of Kerry (Oidhreacht,
 Ballyheigue 1991)
Con Greaney: Traditional Singer (Oidhreacht, Ballyheigue 1991)
Homecoming/An Bealach 'na Bhaile (selected poems of Cathal Ó Searcaigh)
 — Cló Iar Chonnachta, Conamara 1993
Irish Poetry Now: Other Voices (Wolfhound Press, Dublin 1993)
Kerry Through Its Writers (New Island Books, Dublin 1993)
*The Listowel Literary Phenomenon: North Kerry Writers — A Critical
 Introduction* (Cló Iar Chonnachta, Conamara 1994)

THE VILLAGE SINGS

poems by

GABRIEL FITZMAURICE

STORY LINE PRESS
PETERLOO POETS
CLÓ IAR-CHONNACHTA
1996

Story Line Press, Three Oaks Farm, Brownsville, OR 97327
ISBN 1-885266-29-4 $ 9.00

Peterloo Poets, 2 Kelly Gardens, Calstock, Cornwall PL18 9SA, U. K.
ISBN 1-871471-61-3 £ 6.95

Cló Iar-Chonnachta, Indreabhán, Conamara, Co. na Gaillimhe, Éire
ISBN 1-900693-14-3 IR £ 6.95

This publication was made possible thanks in part to the generous support of the Nicholas Roerich Museum, the Andrew W. Mellon Foundation, the National Endowment for the Arts, and our individual contributors.

Book design by Chiquita Babb
Cover Illustration: Sean nós Singer *by Bob O'Cathail, Ballintlea, Ventry, Co. Kerry, Ireland*

Library of Congress Cataloging-in-Publication Data
Fitzmaurice, Gabriel, 1952–
    The village sings : poems / by Gabriel Fitzmaurice.
       p. cm.
    ISBN 1-885266-29-4
    1. Ireland—Poetry. I. Title.
PR6056.I87V54 1996
    821'.914—dc20   96-20631
                        CIP

ACKNOWLEDGEMENTS

Acknowledgements are due to the following where several of these poems have been published or broadcast:

An Ríocht '93 (Kerry Association in Dublin Yearbook), *Europa* (Leuven, Belgium), *Knockanure Pattern 1840–1990, Letters* (Leuven-in Dutch translation), *Lifelines 2, Poetry Ireland Review,* Radio Kerry (Déardaoin, Poetry Matters, The Rambling House), RTE Radio 1 (A Sense of Place, The Gay Byrne Hour, Inprint, Playback, The Arts Show, The Open Mind), RTE Television (The Late Late Show, Summer Signpost, The Pure Drop), *Shannonside Journal* 1994 (Asdee), *Stet* (Cork), *The Applegarth Review* (Moyvane), *The Ballyguiltenane Rural Journal* (Glin), *The Clifden Anthology, The North Kerry Chronicle* (Listowel), *The Salmon* (Galway), *The Spectator* (London), *The Steeple* (Cork), *The Sunday Tribune* (Dublin).

Acknowledgement is due to Beaver Row Press for permission to reprint "The Hurt Bird" from *Road to the Horizon* (Beaver Row Press 1987) and "Getting to Know You" and "Dancing Through" from *Dancing Through* (Beaver Row Press 1990).

Acknowledgement is due to Wolfhound Press for permission to reprint "The Hurt Bird" and "Getting to Know You" from *Irish Poetry Now: Other Voices* (Wolfhound Press 1993).

Acknowledgement is due to New Island Books for permission to reprint "Hence the Songs," "Galvin and Vicars" and "Port na bPúcaí" from *A Kerry Suite* from *Kerry Through Its Writers* (New Island Books 1993).

Several of these poems appeared on my cassette tape *The Space Between: New and Selected Poems 1984–1992* (Cló Iar Chonnachta 1992) and in the accompanying book (Cló Iar Chonnachta 1993). "Getting to Know You," "Dancing Through," and "Galvin and Vicars" appeared on the CD *'Blaiseadh'* (Cló Iar Chonnachta 1995). Acknowledgement is gratefully made.

CONTENTS

Eight Sonnets

For Nessa, with love.

NOT FOR SALE

HENCE THE SONGS

i.m. Billy Cunningham, singer

How soon great deeds are abstract . . .

Hence the songs —
The mighty deeds the tribe sings in the bar:
Gaisce diminished by the video.

Men I never knew still star
In North Kerry Finals,
Their deeds not history but myth
Alive upon a singer's breath;

Again local men are martyred
In a lonely glen;

Now love is lost,
A Rose is won —

Things insufficient till they're sung . . .

Gaisce: (Irish) valour, great exploits, boasting.

GALVIN AND VICARS

i.m. Mick Galvin, killed in action, Kilmorna,
Knockanure (in the parish of Newtown Sandes,
now Moyvane) on Thursday, 7 April, 1921;

Sir Arthur Vicars, shot at Kilmorna House, his
residence, on Thursday, 14 April, 1921.

Mick Galvin, Republican,
Arthur Vicars, who knows what?
— Some sort of Loyalist —
In Ireland's name were shot:

Vicars by Republicans,
Galvin by the *Tans*,
Both part of my history —
The parish of Newtown Sandes

Named to flatter landlords
(But 'Moyvane' today,
Though some still call it 'Newtown' —
Some things don't go away

Easily). Galvin and Vicars,
I imagine you as one —
Obverse and reverse
Sundered by the gun.

History demands
We admit each other's wrongs:
Galvin and Vicars,
Joined only in this song,

Nonetheless I join you
In the freedom of this state
For art discovers symmetries
Where politics must wait.

TWO BROTHERS

Two brothers joined the Column
To fight for *Ireland Free*,
Then the Treaty divided them;
The story that united
Shattered with the dream:
A man without a story
Is a man who must redeem himself.
The community of purpose
Shattered like a glass,
Each seeing his own image
Singly, piece by piece
Where once all life was mirrored;
He would again be whole —
Fighting for their stories,
Comrades, brothers, soldiers
Join in Civil War
And so did these two brothers.
They never again shared
Sleep beneath the same roof,
A pint in any bar,
Dinner at one table.
And so, the fighting over,
They both moved to the Bronx,
Married, raised families —
Never once
Did they communicate.
I remember as a child
Their (separate) Summer visits,
Two storied men who smiled at me
And played my childish games:
I remember with affection,
At times recite their names

When opposite *is* opposite.
Some things won't unite:
Wounds will knit, not stories
Till the poetry is right.

Column: i.e. *Flying Column*, an active service unit of the I.R.A. during the War
of Independence.

SURVIVOR

Captain, I remember you
Praying every day
At the statue of Saint Anthony
For the men you shot. They

Haunted you in your old age
To your asylum — prayer:
This faith that once divided you,
That fought a Civil War

To forge order from division,
Sustained you, though the state
That both sides fought for
Neither could create;

But, for all that, a Republic
Where you played the Captain's part
Biting every bullet,
Knowing in your heart

That, though the war is over
And we vote in liberty,
There's a *Britain* in all of us
From which we're never free.

AMONG THE NATIONS

"... Let no man write my epitaph; for as no man who knows my motives dare now vindicate them, let not prejudice or ignorance asperse them. Let them and me rest in obscurity and peace, and my tomb remain uninscribed, and my memory in oblivion, until other times and other men can do justice to my character. When my country takes her place among the nations of the earth, then, and not till then, let my epitaph be written."

from Robert Emmet's *Speech from the Dock*, 19 September, 1803.

Stanley, I feel I know you,
Contrairy to the end —
A public entertainment,
A soul without a friend;

An accidental patriot
— Jailed in Ireland's cause
For singing 'seditious ballads'
Contrary to law.

You shrugged off opportunity,
Shunned the hero's name —
The perks it would have brought you,
You didn't care to claim;

For what was Independence?
— A fabulous regime,
Yet a state you could have sung against
And still be no *shoneen*.

Freedom is a state of mind
That none can plot or graph —
Uncle, devil's advocate,
This is your epitaph.

*to the memory of my grand-uncle,
Mick Foran ("Stanley")*

Contrairy: Hiberno-English roughly corresponding to the English 'contrary';
P.W. Joyce defines it in his *English As We Speak It In Ireland* as "cross, perverse,
cranky, crotchety."

Shoneen: (Hiberno-English) contemptuously refers to an Irish person aping
English ways; there is a hint of betrayal in the word.

GAEILGE

for Micheál Ó Conghaile

I was wild and wonderful
With many dialects —
Erratic, individual
As the genius that expressed

Itself through me;
On my terms suitors wooed —
I revealed to those who pleased me
My hidden voice and mood.

I was Queen of dialect
And language through me sang
Like poetry, the thrill
Of words upon my tongue.

I gave myself to language —
We agreed like rhyme,
Different yet harmonious.
Widowed now by time,

Dependent on the grammar
Prescribed for me — this crutch;
Doctored by officials
Who care about as much

For wilderness and wonder
As a Civil Servant's Form,
Oh for the tongue of passion!
To be swept again by storm!

Gaeilge: the Irish language.

HIRING TIME AT THE SUPERMARKET

for Cathy Callan

They take you in and tell you how to smile,
Label you to show you're left your name,
Tell you who to court; and on your file —
The things you are not told, the trump of blame . . .

NOT FOR SALE

for Tomáisín Ó Cíobháin, artist

Images of his *Gaeltacht*
—That state we often veil—
Are offered by the artist.
One is not for sale.

So this is the real *Gaeltacht*
And money has no worth
Before the re-creation
Of the native earth.

It hangs there, democratic—
For none, and so for all,
The conscience of creation
In oils upon the wall.

Gaeltacht: (Irish) an Irish-speaking district; the state of being Irish.

TAKING STOCK

Homage to Con Greaney, singer

The true test of the artist
Is that he perseveres;
Today the *sean-nós* singer
Sounds strange to ears

Raised on western harmony,
Plastic and the car,
Antiques to reassure us
In bungalow and bar;

For the times they are a-changin'
Never mind the consequence
Only hypocrites and innocents
Complain about events

(And earth and air and water
— That mirror of health
Reflecting in their wholesomeness
How we regard ourselves . . .)

Driving to the studio,
Con Greaney by my side,
Antiques are for the guilty —
Tradition, like him, rides

Between two cultures.
Sure! there is a price
— My Mazda's part of it,
The studio too (Con's voice

Captured for posterity)
As we ride the middle way
Between selling out and buying in
Sufficient for the day.

Sean-nós: (Irish) old custom; traditional singing.

FROM THE IRISH

THE YELLOW BITTERN

Bitter, bird, it is to see
After all your spree, your bones stretched, dead;
Not hunger — No! by thirst laid low,
Flattened here on the back of your head.
It's worse than the ruin of Troy to me
To see you stretched among bare rock
Who never did harm nor treachery
Preferring water to finest hock.

My lovely bird, I sorely grieve
To see you stretched beside my path
Where you would swill and drink your fill
And from the puddle I'd hear your rasp.
Everyone warns your brother Cathal
That the drink will kill him, to stop and think;
But that's not so — observe this crow
Lately dead for want of drink.

My youthful bird, I'm so depressed
To see you stretched among the gorse
And the rats assembling for your waking
To sport and pleasure by your corpse.
And if you'd only sent a message
That you were in a fix, and dry,
I'd have split the ice upon Lake Vesey,
You'd have wet your mouth and your craw inside.

It's not for these birds that I'm mourning,
The blackbird, songthrush or the crane
But my yellow bittern, a hearty fellow,
Like me in colour, habit, name.

He was ever drinking, drinking
And so am I (they say I'm cursed)—
There's no drop I'm offered that I won't scoff
For fear that I might die of thirst.

"Give up the booze," my darling begs me,
"'Twill be your death." Not so, I think;
I correct my dear's delusion—
I'll live longer the more I'll drink.
Look at this smooth-throated tippler
Dead from drought beside me here—
Good neighbours all, come wet your whistles
For in the grave you'll drink no beer.

*from the Irish of Cathal Buí Mac Giolla Ghunna
(c. 1690–1756).*

THE SPAILPÍN FÁNACH

Never more will I go to Cashel
To pawn or wreck my health,
Nor back the wall at the Hiring Fair
Hanging 'round for the deal to be dealt —
Bigwigs of farmers on their high horses
Hiring the broad and the brawny:
Oh! It's off we must go though the journey be far;
Here's off with the *Spailpín Fánach*.

A *Spailpín Fánach* I was left,
Depending on my vigour,
To walk the early morning dew
Contracting three-month shivers.
No sickle in my hand to reap,
No flail, no spade I'll handle,
But France's colours o'er my bed
And a pike there, too, for battle.

When in Callan with hook in hand,
I'm head of all the mowing,
In *Dúilinn* "Here's the *Spailpín*"
I hear the locals crowing;
But I'll get sense and head for home,
Spend time with Mom, the darling,
And never more will I be called
By my own "The *Spailpín Fánach*."

Farewell, farewell, my father's land,
Sweet Castleisland too,
To the blades of Cool who'll stand on guard
When times require them to.

But now in places foreign to me,
These regions I am thrall in,
I rue the day that I set out
To roam, a *Spailpín Fánach.*

How well I mind my people
Who at Gale Bridge once counted
Their cattle, sheep, white sucky calves,
Whose horses there were mounted;
But evicted, 'twas Christ's will,
We left, our health we hawked-in —
It breaks my heart whene'er I hear
"Call here, you *Spailpín Fánach.*"

If the French were coming o'er the sea
And their bold regiments sailing,
And the Buck O'Grady safely home
And poor, kind Tadgh O'Daly,
We'd raze the Barracks of the King
And yeomen, too, we'd slaughter:
Yes! Irishmen would lay them low —
That'd help the *Spailpín Fánach.*

from the Irish of Ó Brosnacháin?
(late 18th Century?)

Spailpín Fánach: (Irish) a wandering agricultural labourer (pronounce *Spalpeen
Fawn-uck*).

CILL AODÁIN

Now Spring is upon us, the days will be stretching,
And after *The Biddy*, I'll hoist up and go;
Since I've decided, there'll be no returning
Till I stand in the middle of County Mayo.
In the town of Claremorris I'll spend the first evening,
And in Balla below it, the first drinks will flow,
Then to Kiltimagh travel to spend a whole month there
Barely two miles from Ballinamore.

I set down forever that my spirit rises
Like fog as it scatters, as wind starts to blow
When I'm thinking of Carra or Balla below it,
Or Scahaveela or the plain of Mayo.
Cill Aodáin the fertile, where all fruits are growing —
Blackberries, raspberries, full-fruited each one,
And if I were standing among my own people
The years they would leave me, again I'd be young.

from the Irish of Antoine Ó Reachtabhra
(c. 1784–1835).

The Biddy: Saint Brigid's Day, the first day of Spring.
Cill Aodáin: (pronounce *Kill Ay-dawn*) was the poet's place of birth.

I AM RAFTERY

I am Raftery the poet
Of hope and love,
With eyes without light
Calm, untroubled.

In the light of my heart
Retracing my way,
Worn and weary
To the end of my days.

Look at me now,
My back to a wall,
Playing music
For empty pockets.

from the Irish of Antoine Ó Reachtabhra.

MARY MOST GRACE-FULL

Mary most grace-full,
mother of Christ,
guard me and guide me
all of my life.

Keep me, I beg you,
from each evil rôle;
save, I beseech you,
my body and soul.

Guard me from ocean,
on dry land as well;
keep me, my mother,
safe from hell.

Above me, guardian
Seraphim;
God before me,
God within.

traditional.

THE VILLAGE
SCHOOLMASTER

"Beside yon straggling fence that skirts the way,
With blossom'd furze unprofitably gay,
There, in his noisy mansion, skilled to rule,
The village master taught his little school.
A man severe he was, and stern to view;
I knew him well, and every truant knew:
Well had the boding tremblers learned to trace
The day's disasters in his morning face;
Full well they laughed with counterfeited glee
At all his jokes, for many a joke had he;
Full well the busy whisper circling round
Conveyed the dismal tidings when he frowned.
Yet he was kind, or, if severe in aught,
The love he bore to learning was in fault;
The village all declared how much he knew:
'Twas certain he could write, and cypher too;
Lands he could measure, terms and tides presage,
And e'en the story ran that he could gauge:
In arguing, too, the parson owned his skill,
For e'en though vanquished, he could argue still;
While words of learned length and thundering sound
Amazed the gazing rustics ranged around;
And still they gazed, and still the wonder grew,
That one small head could carry all he knew."

Oliver Goldsmith (1728–1774)
from "The Deserted Village"

THE ROAD TO DAMASCUS

She looks me squarely in the eye
And says (no trace of fright),
"You think you're the biggest man in the world,"
And, to my shame, she's right.

I persecute with learning,
Make her, and others, fail
In the name of education.
It's I, not she, who've failed.

This, then, is the moment,
Struck from my high horse,
I see the child before me —
Child most wondrous.

She looks at me, offended,
Her accusation mild.
Who would become a teacher
Must first become a child . . .

THE INTERVIEW

"How would you sell yourself as a teacher?"
What can I say but a teacher's not for sale,
That our choice of word often will betray us;
She's interested, but I can see I've failed

To convince her of the value of this reading,
That, a teacher, I am bound to pass along
The values inherent in our language,
Values I'd inculcate in the young.

I could if I would blow my own trumpet,
Dazzle with achievement — then she'd see
What selling is, and all of pence and ha'pence,
But I'm suspicious she's not opened my C.V.

This, then, is the system that I work for —
Blessed are the glib for they shall gain;
"What profit it a man to gain the world . . ."
I whisper to myself to keep me sane.

2-D, 3-D

for Fintan O'Toole

Today in class was time for shape —
Squares and cubes,
2-D, 3-D.

To elicit interest
I speak of 3-D glasses for television:
"Did you ever see a horror-movie in 3-D?"
I ask.

One child describes his brother's fall from a chair
As he ducked a knife thrown on television
While he was wearing 3-D glasses.

Another follows suit
Improvising a make-believe of horror-videos and knives
But I'd need 3-D glasses to believe him.

He sees his story as it unfolds,
Needs me to approve a world that proving will destroy;
He invites me to this world
And I enter.

I look back in through my own two eyes —
So much that I must realize:
To cube it truly is the test.

More is than there is manifest.

THE LONE STAR TRAIL

for Gerard Quinn

It started as a song—
A simple round
Of cowboys and of cattle

Till sound possessed the children
Who yelled
And neighed
And mooed:

Cowboy was a horse
And both were cattle.

Then the song became their pictures
Swift and rude.

They offer me their pictures for approval
(All suns and no horizons) . . .

I approve.

'THE FREE BOOKS'

for Chriss Nolan

No books and it's October,
Five weeks since school began —
Excuses since September,
Doing what he can

With no books to study
(No homework — wow! that's cool!),
A little boy who's ready
To do his best at school.

His Daddy is redundant,
He drinks his dole at home,
His Mammy's out at Bingo
And Sonny is alone;

The Lotto, lucky numbers,
The miracle they pray for —
They do it religiously every week
(A let-down that they pay for).

Here, Sonny, are your school books,
A chance, for you, my son;
Here is your book of numbers —
Let's open on page one . . .

THE HURT BIRD

After playtime
Huddled in the classroom . . .

In the yard
Jackdaws peck the ice
While the class guesses
The black birds:

Blackbirds?
(Laughter).

Crows?
Well yes . . .
But jackdaws.
Those are jackdaws.
Why do they peck the ice?

Wonder
Becomes jackdaws' eyes
Rummaging the ice
Till suddenly
At the window opposite

— Oh the bird!
The poor bird!

At the shout
The jackdaws fright.

Sir, a robin sir . . .
He struck the window

And he fell
And now he's dying
With his legs up
On the ice:

The jackdaws
Will attack it sir,

They will rip its puddings out.

I take the wounded bird,
Deadweight
In my open palm
—No flutter
No escaping

And lay it
On the floor near heat,
The deadweight
Of the wound
Upon my coat.

Grasping
The ways of pain,
The pain of birds
They cannot name,
The class are curious
But quiet:

They will not frighten
The struggle of death and living.

Please sir,
Will he die?

And I
Cannot reply.

Alone
With utter pain

Eyes closed

The little body
Puffed and gasping

Lopsided yet upright:

He's alive,
The children whisper
Excited
As if witnessing
His birth.

Would he drink water sir?
Would he eat bread?
Should we feed him?

Lopsided
The hurt bird
With one eye open
To the world
Shits;

He moves
And stumbles.

I move
To the hurt bird:

The beak opens
—For food
Or fight?

I touch
The puffed red breast
With trepid finger;

I spoon water
To the throat:

It splutters.

Children crumb their lunches
Pleading
To lay the broken bread
Within reach of the black head.

The bird
Too hurt to feed
Falls in the valley
Of the coat,
And as I help
It claws
And perches on my finger

Bridging the great divide
Of man and bird.

He hops
From my finger
To the floor

And flutters
Under tables
Under chairs

Till exhausted
He tucks his head
Between wing and breast
Private
Between coat and wall.

The class
Delights in silence
At the sleeping bird.

The bird sir . . .
What is it —
A robin?
—Look at the red breast.

But you never see a robin
With a black head.

I tell them
It's a bullfinch
Explaining the colours why;

I answer their questions
From the library.

And the children draw the bullfinch

—With hurt
And gasp
And life

—With the fearlessness of pain
Where the bird will fright

And in the children's pictures
Even black and grey
Are bright.

GETTING TO KNOW YOU

Thomas,
You don't trust me —
I can tell from your trapped eyes.
How can I help you,
My sulky friend?
Tell you I love you?
(That would seem like lies).
To reach out to touch you
Might offend.

Give you your head;
Watch over
In so far as any human can;
Coax you with tacit kindness;
Greet you, man to man . . .

Yes, Thomas,
I am strong
(But equal) —
And, Thomas,
We are both 'at school':
Both circling round
A common understanding,
Both sniffing at the smile
That sweetens rules.

Today you bounce up to me,
Your eyes the rising sun:

We share your secret story —

Hello!
God bless you,
Tom . . .

THE OLD WORDS

for Deirdre Shanahan

They've left our mouths this generation,
They'll pass from mind the next,
Old words that were a way of life
Which can't now be expressed.

The old words are out on pension,
A new world's being said:
When words become redundant,
Their voice, their world is dead.

A *kippen* sounds a *kitten*
In the world where I teach;
I bring a *gabháil* of old words
To my class that I might reach

Perhaps one boy or girl
Who'll pick them up for fun —
Words of generation,
World that is gone . . .

kippen: from the Irish *cipín*, a little stick
gabháil: (Irish) an armful (pronounce *gu-awl*)

PRIMARY EDUCATION

He put on the blues this morning,
Blue shirt, v-neck, blue tie—
The stamp of conformity
(His own clothes would defy

The system we impose on him—
He can't wear what he will:
How different is a uniform
To our desire to kill

The little spark of genius
That makes us different?);
In my schooldays, I remember,
Everybody went

Dressed as they had clothes to wear—
Those of us with shoes
And underpants were "cissies";
If we could, we'd choose

The bare feet, short pants, no "knickers"
Of the jealous tots-to-twelves
For freedom isn't granted,
We win it from ourselves.

MANNA IN
THE STREET

THE COMMON TOUCH

for Robert McDowell

Perky Nolan was a stuck-up dog —
The schoolmaster's.
He never fought with the other dogs that held the street.
He was manicured as street-urchins would never be.

Perky went for *walkies* with the master's daughter,
Manicured as herself.
Beside her, Perky tiptoed like a dancer;
He cocked his leg, important as the Anthem in Croke Park;
He cocked his nose, a *mammy's boy*,
And broadcast with his bark.

Perky was all things a villager would never be,
And so the village waited . . .

One day Perky got loose and walked free;
The village nosed him.
Perky made a show of baring teeth,
But there was no harm in him.

This was the chance we'd waited for . . .

"Perky! Here boy! Here boy!
Good dog! Good dog!"
We called, holding out our hands.
Perky sniffed and padded towards us.

"Kick the shit out of him boys," we exploded.

Shoes, boots, wellingtons and bare toes thudded into him.

He howled and ran:

"That'll teach him to put on airs," the village gloated.

Perky found the common touch —
The same for dog and man.

NARCISSUS

"I'll be your friend forever"
Means it's time to part;
She thinks she means 'forever' —
She hasn't got the heart

To spell it out quite plainly
That she wants his love no more,
That she finds his kisses sloppy,
His company a bore.

He doesn't want this friendship —
He needs her all the way,
For love of her, he turns a cur,
He'll lie and he'll betray

Everyone who loves him
For love of what's refused,
And every song is of his wrong
When he's wallowing in booze.

He thinks he loves her: he does not —
His love of self is great
(This is what he sees in her);
Without her, much self-hate . . .

THAT CHRISTMAS

I won't forget that Christmas,
The one when Cud was drowned
And I was on the edge myself
And Cud was never found.

His car parked by the river —
Did he leave or dive?
And always the snap sighting
That Cud was still alive.

No body could we bury,
No Requiem for him,
No chance to say "I'm sorry
For your trouble" to his kin.

That Christmas on the river
We placed boulders on the rim —
An obstacle to suicide
(For cars were driven in . . .)

I won't forget that Christmas,
The Christmas of the crane,
Cars hauled from the river,
The village numb with pain.

ODE TO A BLUEBOTTLE

It never is quite summer
Till you fizz around the room,
Drone to summer's chanter,
Spurt, a loosed balloon.

It never is quite summer
Till you're splattered on the sill:
Oh, we don't want all of summer.
Much of it we kill.

BUDGIE

"Which budgie do you want, John?"
The one what's white and blue.
Dad! He'll be lonely on his own —
We should get another too."

I ask the bird-man if we should;
He shakes his head and grins
At well-intentioned ignorance.
"A budgie," he begins,

"Must have no companions;
The only way he'll talk
Is separate from others"
(The budgie in me baulks);

"Otherwise he'll only chirp —
He'll never say a word;
You must keep him on his own."
(The poet as a bird . . .)

He puts some seed and water,
A mirror in the cage
And underneath the sparkling bars
A virgin foolscap page . . .

TOM COOPER

for John and Josie Sweeney

It's not the name has meaning
But the thing-that-has-a-name;
Consider one Tom Cooper
From our childhood days,

The *Urney* chocolate logo
(Was it?) — the elf who grinned
On the paper wrapper.
We never thought of him

Till, named by Paddy Sweeney
To divert his young son John
Who plagued his Dad for chocolate,
Tom Cooper began.

Tom Cooper, Paddy told him,
Made chocolate out of turf —
There were no bars the evenings
That he ran out of turf!

Unnamed, he had no meaning;
He lived up to his name —
The only limits on him
What one could entertain.

Conceived out of necessity
— To imagine, therefore gain —
How much of life's invented
Created by its name . . .

WITH MICHAEL HARTNETT
IN BARNAGH GARDENS

August 22, 1993

I know that you're not here, dear Mike,
In spirit or in flesh,
And all I fancy cannot change
The fact that it's myself

That feels you here on Barnagh
As wasps *om* through the day
And *Coke* attracts their zig-zag jabs
Among the kids at play.

These wasps? No! They're not *om*ing —
They're buzzing as they fly;
It's just a shaper's mind, Mike,
That sees them with an eye

That draws all things together
And makes them what they're not
And yet that sees them as they are.
Each one his own poet,

We filter out our present
Through muslin of our lives —
Do wasps on Barnagh buzz or *om?*
Experience decides . . .

AN OLD MAN AND HIS JOY

Today I saw pain's beauty
In an old man and his joy —
His brain-damaged grandson.
(For years I'd passed them by;

The old man would support him
And clap his grandson's hands,
But I had no children then
And didn't understand).

Propped up, protected in the old man's arms,
The boy shambled down the street,
And, while he gave no smile, no sign
(Nothing that I could see),

I felt the care between them.
Though life needs anodyne,
I'm grateful for this beauty.
I suffer it as mine.

THY WILL BE DONE

for Dennis O'Driscoll

The old man in Coronary Care
Calmly tells his beads,
His fingers white as candles.
Here no ego pleads

With the Virgin of the Rosary
To prolong his days;
Ignoring my attention,
Thy Will be done, he prays . . .

WILLIE DORE

Willie Dore was simple,
He smelled. The village fool,
He lived alone among the rats
In a shack below the school.

Two rats' eyes in his leather face
Stabbed out beneath the layer
Of dirt that blackened him like soot.
He wasn't born *quare*,

But some disease the doctor
Couldn't cure (or name)
Trapped him in his childhood
Hobbling his brain.

Willie Dore was a happy man
Though peevish as a huff—
He fed, he drank, he slept, he rose,
He dreamed—that was enough . . .

Each sausage scrounged from a travelling van
Was a vital victory;
Each penny coaxed from a passing priest
Was a cunning comedy.

Willie never knew his age—
No matter how you'd pry,
"The one age to Mary Mack"
Was all he could reply.

He lived as he imagined,
Saw manna in the street,
Eighty years of scavenging,
Admitting no defeat.

quare: (dialect) a version of 'queer,' meaning 'strange,' 'unusual,' 'mentally un-balanced.'

THE VILLAGE HALL

The old Hall with its shaky stage
Was good enough for us —
Bill Horan and Eileen Manaher
Wholly marvellous

As they called up here before us
A world of their own,
The magic I have grown to love,
The farce I loved, outgrown.

The queue outside the musty Hall,
The key turned in the lock,
The stampede to the benches,
The fizz, the sweets, clove rock;

And then the silence as the play
Took us in its spell,
Local folk turned Gods and Queens
In this miracle.

The Hall is old, not worth repair,
They'll knock it, build anew;
My boy and girl will taste in there
The magic that I knew;

They'll find the things a village finds
In the local Hall —
That as Eileen becomes a Queen
We're not ourselves at all.

OUT OF THE
ORDINARY

DANCING THROUGH

Homage to Mikey Sheehy, footballer

Nureyev with a football,
You solo to the goal
Where the swell of expectation
Spurts in vain —
O master of the ritual,
O flesh of tribal soul,
Let beauty be at last
Released from pain . . .

Now grace eludes its marker
Creating its own space
While grim defenders
Flounder in its wake;
And the ball you won from conflict
Yields to your embrace —
Goal beckons like a promise . . .
And you take.

AT THE BALL GAME

for Seamus Heaney

Everything out there you see
'S a version of reality
As heroes triumph over doubt
And bring their kind of truth about.

Each, according to his way,
Engages on the field of play,
And, urging on, the faithful crowd
Are cheering, praising, cursing loud
For beauty only will suffice,
Beauty to infuse our lives:
No cup, no trophy will redeem
Victory by ignoble means.

And, so, we take the field today
To find ourselves in how we play,
Out there on the field to be
Ourselves, a team, where all can see;
For nothing is but is revealed
And tested on the football field.

FIREPLACE

Where nothing was
But space alone
A fireplace is
Revealed in stone

Which shapes and garlands
The hearth's void —
The empty centre.
With what pride

The mason smiles
Who has let be
The perfect
Possibility . . .

PORT NA bPÚCAÍ

for Tony Mac Mahon

'Music of the Fairies' —
I wonder what he knew:
He heard a world and named it;
Came back to tell it, too.

Possessed by so-called 'fairies,'
The fiddler had to find
A beauty that would please him
As they played upon his mind.

'Music of the Fairies' —
Like any poet he knew
That beauty would destroy him
Unless he made it, too . . .

Port na bPúcaí: (Irish) 'The Fairies' Music,' a Blasket Island air. It was believed to have been heard from the fairies and translated to the fiddle by a Blasket fiddler. It has been suggested that the air is based on the call of a seal (or a whale) heard that night off *Inis Icíleáin,* the most southerly of the Blaskets.

BLESSÈD ASHES

Nellie lived on Main Street
In a thatched hut with her cats;
A lady given much to prayer,
She never washed.
The cats were wild to everyone
But herself —
When she went to hospital
The cats ran off.

They cleaned her up in hospital —
Powder, manicure.
Nellie hated cleanliness:
When she got inside her door,
She missed her cats,
Her house was clean,
The fire was lit.

She shuffled out the back door
To the ash-pit;
She rubbed ashes in her hair.

Nellie returned, radiant
For ash to her was prayer.

MARY

Hail, full of grace
The Angel, uninvited,
Came to you in your own place
And your word united

Heaven and Earth, Above, Below —
God needed you to say
Behold Thy handmaid; had you said *No,*
Where was God today?

A plucky girl, unmarried too
At the time of this conception —
What some would do to such as you
Does not bear mention.

You took your chance on God and life
No man before your will,
Queen of Heaven, common wife,
No precious, pale rel-

igious thing,
No prop for those who would
Impose themselves on everything
Not least your womanhood.

NATIVITY

Augustus Caesar had decreed
That all the world should be counted,
The Empire's business must proceed —
His subjects taxed, the taxes mounted . . .

At this decree, the people travelled
To be numbered with their clan,
And thus the prophesies unravelled —
The Word Made Flesh, the Son of Man
Was born in a stable
In David's city, Bethlehem,
No silver spoon, no cot, no cradle,
Because there was no room for Him
In Inn or Hostel, B&B —
There was no room, there was no bed,
And profit couldn't find a key
To shelter Christ, and so instead
In a stable He was born
And laid into a manger —
How settled folk dismiss with scorn
The family they deem a stranger.

But on a hill outside the town
While shepherds watched, these outdoor men,
Their minds were opened with the sound
Of their perception; it came to them
That Angels told, "In the town below,
In a manger you'll find laid
Where asses bray and oxen low
A new King born." The shepherds made
Off at once and left their sheep,

And found between a cow and mare
The infant Jesus fast asleep,
Put coin in hand, their worldly share.

Jesus wakes, chucks the coin away;
Joseph retreives it from the hay.

"I THIRST"

Midnight Mass one Christmas Eve,
The Parish comes to pray —
A midnight of nostalgia
After a hard day;

For some have been preparing
Their Christmas at the sink,
And others have spent the day
Revelling in drink.

At Midnight Mass, the Parish
Bows its head in prayer —
All but one have come along
In pious posture there.

All day, he's been drinking
In *The Corner House*;
When it comes to closing time
He buys, to carry out
For after Mass, two bottles
Of Guinness Extra Stout.

And he stands there with the others
At the back wall of the Church;
When it comes to the Offertory,
Suddenly with a lurch

He staggers up the centre aisle
While the crowd looks on in shock,
Halting at the altar rails,
Careful not to drop

The bottles, he takes them out,
Plants them on the rails,
Faces the congregation,
Waves and then repairs

To the back and anonymity,
Hitches up his arse,
And some are shocked, and some amused
At this unholy farce.

But the Christ who thirsts on Calvary
Has waited all these years
For a fellow cursed with the cross of thirst
To stand him these few beers.

MOMENTS WHEN HOPELESSNESS IS PHYSICAL

Moments when hopelessness is physical,
When strength deserts and blackness hoods my eyes,
When ferrets are uncaged and hunt within me
With a fierceness no drug can tranquillize;
When God is neither good nor a protector,
When lover, parents, friends no longer care,
I have toppled from the sturdy tower of logic
Thrashing in the reservoir of prayer.

And I, who was always a poor swimmer
Soon to tire, would falter and go down —
Where Peter's faith could walk upon the water
All I can do is cry "I drown! I drown!"
Then a hand, a blessed hand, around my shoulder
Keeps my head above the water, pulls me in:
What logic cannot call — this Guardian Angel,
This second nature rises from within.

GOOD FRIDAY

Good Friday was the day of periwinkles:
The only day we got them—oh, the treat!
An old lady and her son came up from Bally
With an assload. They were much more fun than meat.

They sold them by the handful to us children;
We took them home and pestered Mom for pins.
They looked like snots when you fished them out. But Jesus!
That was some way to atone for all your sins!

We ate them by the fistful all that morning,
Receiving the essence of the tide.
The empty shells prefigured eggs for Easter.
At three o'clock the Christ was crucified.

The tang of winkles flavours my Good Fridays,
The emptiness familiar as the day.
The old woman's dead, her son too. Every weekend
The winkle man revives them on his tray.

IN MEMORIAM DANNY CUNNINGHAM 1912-1995

I take her to the Funeral Home —
She wants to see him dead;
She's not afraid — she rubs his hands
And then explores his head.

"He not wake up I rub him.
Look, Daddy! He not move.
Where Danny, Dad?" she asks me.
"Danny's dead, my love."

"Where Danny, Dad?" she asks again;
Then suddenly it's clear —
"The old Danny in the box," she says;
The new one — he not here."

OISÍN'S FAREWELL TO NIAMH

No-one can live forever
And even if we could
We'd choose death in the long run.
This is good.

Tír na nÓg's for children —
Nothing changes there,
Everyone always smiling,
Flowers in their hair;

And all their songs are child's songs
Where nothing ever grows,
But to a poet and soldier,
To such a one as knows

The death-and-birth of seasons,
Though Eternal Youth's his bride,
Such a one must live his life,
Such a one can't hide

In eternal youth and happiness
Where nothing ever dies —
Once you've lived with mortals,
Tír na nÓg is lies.

So fare thee well, my Princess,
I must leave you now, my dear,
Back to death in Ireland
To face my fear.

Tír na nÓg: (Irish) The Land of Eternal Youth

EIGHT SONNETS

for John B. Keane

ART WITHOUT OPINION

for George Szirtes

Art without opinion, the arts page tells us—
Passwords, I suspect, of coterie;
A wild man in the desert, rude, rebellious,
I live by art—the art of being me.
This is what the dealers try to sell us:
That nothing *is* outside their tyranny.
He who has submitted is most jealous
Pinned and wriggling in the gallery.

This horror of the subject is absurd,
The art of no opinion is afraid;
Art is its own critic—like a bird,
It sings above the shotguns or, instead,
Collapses as a poem may, word by word.
Whatever can be said, let it be said.

BIGWIGS

Bigwigs are self-important as allowed,
Their favours can never be repaid;
They calculate their worth in bank accounts;
Like Royalty, they're born to the grade.
Well-in with all their kind, above the law
That favours power, they'll always get the break;
Their word is always heard, and, though we jaw,
Their influence still holds. How they unmake
Their accusers with a show of power
(The rest are all afraid, or have been bought);
They're overbearing, ignorant and dour
For all attempts upon them come to nought.
They're still around; you can't eradicate
This class, their power, no matter what the state.

A FAMILY TALE

Willie, my mother told me, was *a bad one*—
Everything a good boy shouldn't be:
He wound up in America in prison;
He was the black sheep of our family.
He got married in America to a German—
They lived with her mother in their care;
Willie loved his wife; yes! he was *her* man
(Not her mother's; he threw her down the stairs).
Willie stood for trial, was convicted—
Death Row then to face the electric chair
(The old lady'd died), but how I was uplifted
When I learned what Willie did, how he could dare.
He beat the state before it took its due—
He cut his jugular with an eyelet of his shoe.

THE PULL OF THE SUPERNATURAL

Paddy was a drunk for many years
Like his father and his uncles were before —
He could sink more porter than his peers
Then turn to whiskey when he'd no room for more.
"Life is meant for drinking, not for eating,"
Was the motto he could not articulate —
"We'll go for *one — a small one,*" was his greeting
('One' was never one with him in spate).
One Ash Wednesday, he went off the beer —
"He'll never last," was all that we could say:
We bet on when he'd break out, for 'twas clear
To us he'd not last till Patrick's Day.
He never drank again — invoking dread,
"Paddy musht meet somethin,'" his father said.

musht meet somethin': (colloquial) must have met something from the other-world.

A BEDTIME STORY

I want to give my children what I got—
A sign of middle age and childhood past:
"A story about Daddy—tell us what
You did when you were little—just like us."
What survives our childhood we don't choose—
We must forgive our childhood if we can:
We cannot cite our childhood as excuse—
Hurt is not a license to do wrong.
And so I bring my children to my past,
A past that was unhappy as 'twas good—
A story now, and so my kids have guessed
The happy ending, as indeed they should.
I tuck them in as sleep tugs at their lids.
I hope they'll wish their childhood on their kids.

MAY DALTON

The last word that was left to her was 'honour,'
The stroke had taken all the rest away,
The one thing the void could not take from her
Was herself, and so she used to say
Honour! Honour! Honour! when you addressed her,
Honour! Honour! Honour! while her hand
Clutched her agitation. What depressed her
Was how those closest failed to understand
Honour! Honour! Honour!, how our beaming
Was the beaming of an adult at a child:
Honour! Honour! Honour! had no meaning
For any but May Dalton. So we smiled.
A single word held all she had to say;
Enclosed within this word, she passed away.

THE TEACHER

for David Mason

I wish away my life until the pension
Hoping that, just once, I will connect
With sympathy that is beyond attention;
Instead I keep good order, earn respect.
Once I had a vision for my village —
I'd bring to it a gift of poetry;
Tonight the talk's of quotas and of tillage
And how the barmaid gives out beer for free.
And yet, I've not lost hope in my own people —
My vision was at fault; these people need
To sing and dance, get drunk below the steeple
That accuses them of gossip and of greed.
I mind their children, give them right of way
Into a world I've seen and try to say.

TO MARTIN HAYES, FIDDLER

All that we are given, we can use;
All the notes are there for us to praise —
The tune's set out before us, yet we choose:
The tune evolves in playing. Martin Hayes
Susses out each note before he cues
It; taking thought, he chooses what it says,
Weaves into the fabric his own news:
The tune's predestined, not the way he plays.

The music *is*, the fiddler's taken thought —
All our moments lead to this last *doh*,
All the options, everything that's sought:
What we hear that's played is what we know.
Holy! Holy! Holy! what is wrought!
He raises up, rubs rosin to the bow.